# Can we be good without God?

## John Blanchard

EP Books (Evangelical Press), 1st Floor Venture House, 6 Silver Court, Watchmead, Welwyn Garden City, AL7 1TS

sales@epbooks.org www.epbooks.org

In the USA, EP Books are distributed by:
JPL Fulfillment, 3741 Linden Ave. S.E., Wyoming, MI 49548
Tel: 877–683–6935
order@jplbooks.com www.jplbooks.com

First published 2007
This edition 2016

British Library Cataloguing in Publication Data available

ISBN 978–1–78397–147–3

Unless otherwise indicated, Scripture quotations are from the ESV® Bible (The Holy Bible, English Standard Version®), copyright © 2001 by Crossway, a publishing ministry of Good News Publishers. Used by permission. All rights reserved.
Scripture quotations marked 'NIV' are taken from the Holy Bible, NEW INTERNATIONAL VERSION®, NIV® Copyright © 1973, 1978, 1984, 2011 by Biblica, Inc.® Used by permission.All rights reserved worldwide.

# Can we be good without God?

In December 2005 a film produced in Hollywood and shot mainly in New Zealand swept into Britain on a tidal wave of publicity. Costing $150 million to make, it had already attracted huge audiences in the United States. Now, as it reached the homeland of the author on whose book the screenplay was based, the response was phenomenal, not least from professional film critics. One critic opened his review by saying, 'Here is a wonderful, colossal, stupendous film... This is not just a "must see" but a "must see again and again".' He went on to call the acting quality 'exceptional', the special effects 'breathtaking' and the climax 'truly amazing'. Other newspapers added their enthusiastic endorsements: 'magical', 'enchanting', and 'sensational' were all employed.

Almost as remarkable as the chorus of commendations was the fact that the film had none of the elements often found in modern movies. Although it contained some lively battle scenes, there was no sleaze, no profanity, no salacious sex, no gore and no nudity. Instead, it championed faith and morality.

The film was *The Lion, the Witch and the Wardrobe*, the first of an intended six films based on *The Chronicles of Narnia*, a series of books written by C. S. Lewis some fifty years earlier. In its opening weekend box office takings grossed $67.1 million and attracted rave reviews from coast to coast. The *New York Daily News* rated it 'a thrilling success', the *San Francisco Chronicle* said it was 'a movie of intelligence and power, of beauty, universality and largeness of spirit' and the *Baltimore Sun* called it 'downright ennobling'.

Not everybody agreed. After the film's British premiere the *Guardian's* Polly Toynbee let fly. She found some of it 'toe-curlingly, cringingly awful', saw the whole thing as being 'profoundly manipulative' and 'dark with emotional sadism' and approvingly quoted author Philip Pullman's condemnation of *The Chronicles of Narnia* as 'one of the most ugly, poisonous things I have ever read'. The key to understanding Toynbee's devastating outburst becomes clear at the end of her review, when she attacks the film's central character as 'an emblem for everything an atheist objects to in religion'. She was writing not as an objective film critic, but as a hard-core atheist, convinced that, as we face the constant conflict between good and evil, there is no God to whom we can turn. In her own words, 'No one is watching, no one is guiding, no one is judging and there is no other place yet to come... There is no one here but ourselves to suffer for our sins, no one to redeem us but ourselves... We need no holy guide books, only a very human compass.' This sets the scene perfectly for all that follows in this booklet.

## The starting point

Polly Toynbee's main point is that in the absence of God we are perfectly capable not only of redeeming ourselves from the harmful effects of evil, but of drawing a clear distinction between evil and good in the first place. All we need to make the all-important distinction is 'a very human compass'. But is this the case? Unless God exists, can we even discuss whether anything is 'good' or 'evil'? Do these words have any real meaning unless God is central to our world view? This is the real starting point.

Everyone has a world view, as it simply means the way you look at anything at all—including history, the natural world, your own life and the lives of others. It governs your basic beliefs about all reality, including your total outlook on the universe and your own place in it. Put even more succinctly, a world view is how you view the world. To use a simple illustration, different world views are like people looking at the same scene through differently tinted sunglasses. Your world view influences everything you think, say or do, because it is what you assume to be true before you claim that anything else is true—and it is easy to see that this radically affects your view of ethics and morality.

The word 'ethics' is defined in the *Oxford Dictionary of English* as 'moral principles that govern a person's behaviour or the conducting of an activity', while the same dictionary defines 'morals' as 'standards of behaviour; principles of right and wrong'. The two words are obviously closely related, though their meaning is not strictly identical. In very simple terms, 'morals' *define* what a person believes to be right or wrong, while 'ethics' is *the study of* what a person believes to be right or wrong—and both ethics and morals depend fundamentally on an individual's world view. For example, Polly Toynbee saw exactly the same images and heard exactly the same soundtrack as the critics who praised *The Lion, the Witch and the Wardrobe* to the skies, yet, as the final flourish of her review makes clear, her withering attack was not triggered by a difference in intellect, nationality or cultural prejudice, but by her world view.

For our present purposes we can divide world views into three categories. Firstly, there are those that assume a world without God—such as humanism (man is at the centre of everything), materialism (nature is all there is), existentialism (there are no universal values) and nihilism (nothing is of any ultimate significance). Secondly, there are those tied in to one of the countless religious systems man has invented over the centuries. These range from Hinduism (which offers over thirty million gods) to Zoroastrianism (which says there are two) and include a bewildering cascade of concepts in which God is seen as a force of nature, cosmic energy, a spirit living in all material elements or (as in the case of Islam) as an austere and remote Ruler 'so far above man in every way that he is not personally knowable'. Thirdly, there is the one which sees the God who reveals himself in the Bible not only as the Creator of all reality outside of himself and the sole and sovereign Ruler of all his creation, but as one who created human beings as moral agents, who is passionately concerned for our moral well-being and who calls us into a living relationship with himself. This is the God I have in mind in writing this booklet, and the question we need to ask and answer is this: can we even talk sensibly about good and evil unless this world view governs our thinking?

## Kant's wall

Many of the world's greatest thinkers have wrestled with our question. One of the real heavyweights was the philosopher Immanuel Kant. His 'big idea' was that all knowledge could be divided into two 'worlds'. One comprised the things recognized by our five senses—sight, hearing, smell, taste and touch—while in the other Kant placed God and anything that could not be recognized by our senses or scientifically demonstrated. He then in effect put a 'wall' between these two worlds and said that as human beings we did not have the ability to climb over this wall and get to grips with the second 'world'. It is ironic that whereas his first name—'Immanuel'—is a Hebrew word meaning 'God with us', Kant's teaching has led millions to believe that, far from being 'with us', God is walled up in a world we are unable to reach!

As Kant placed morality on the far side of his 'wall', he was saying that judgements about right and wrong were matters of personal opinion and it is easy to see that Polly Toynbee's 'very human compass' ties in with this idea. Kant's fingerprints are all over the now outdated idea that while science deals only with facts, religion is purely a matter of faith and speculation. Yet even he admitted that there was one area of human experience that *demanded* the existence of God, and an inscription on his tombstone tells us what this was: 'Two things fill my mind with ever new and increasing wonder and awe, the more often and the more intensely the reflection dwells on them, the starry heavens above *and the moral law within*' (emphasis added).

In the course of his writings Kant argued that, as this universal moral law was not something man had invented, it must come from what he called a 'Supreme Being', who gave us freedom to obey or disobey and who would eventually dispense perfect justice beyond the grave. Although his idea of God (an impersonal deity that brought the universe into being and then abandoned it) falls far short of the Bible's teaching, he nevertheless came to the conclusion that 'We must live as though there were a God.' Even this towering sceptic found that he could not build a model of morality without somehow smuggling God into it, as without God the concept of ethics would be meaningless and leave human life without any moral anchor.

### The extra dimension
None of the above is to suggest that people who doubt or deny God's existence are incapable of doing things commonly accepted as being 'good'. This would be a ludicrous idea. As we have already stated, the question we are considering goes much deeper than that and asks what basis we have for describing any thought,

word or action as being 'good' or 'evil' in the first place. For example, in a world without God, can we have any solid reason for calling such things as purity, honesty and humility 'good', or their opposites 'evil'?

The mathematician and humanist Jacob Bronowski once wrote, 'Man is not different in kind from any other forms of life … living matter is not different in kind from dead matter … It seems self-evident to say that man is part of nature, in the same sense that a stone is, or a cactus, or a camel.' This is typical of the views expressed by hard-line atheists, but all the evidence is against it. There are many ways in which human life is fundamentally different not only from the natural world, but from every other form of life on earth. We have vastly superior intelligence; we are historical beings, conscious of our past and concerned about our future; we have a deep-rooted instinct that we are more than atomic accidents; we make unique use of language; we are capable of complex reasoning and lateral thinking; we have mathematical skills; and we have an aesthetic dimension, enabling us to speak of things as being beautiful or ugly.

But humankind has another distinguishing mark, one so universal and entrenched that nobody can honestly or sensibly deny it: *we have a moral dimension*. For thousands of years it has been universally accepted that there is a radical difference between right and wrong, and it seems difficult to deny that a moral law appears to be programmed into our psychological 'software'.

Criminal justice systems would collapse into chaos were this not the case. As C. S. Lewis points out in *Mere Christianity*, 'Human beings, all over the earth, have this curious idea that they ought to behave in a certain way, and cannot get rid of it.' Even though interpretation of a written law may differ from society to society and from individual to individual, it is impossible to deny that on massive moral issues affecting all of humankind there is an overwhelming consensus that is not arrived at by pooling ideas and cobbling together some kind of compromise.

## The intruder

In June 2006 the British press carried a delightful story that illustrated Lewis's claim. Rummaging through an old jacket, eighty-four-year-old John Gedge, from East Sussex, found an unpaid speeding ticket showing that he had been caught driving at 55 mph in a 35 mph zone while on holiday in America in 1954, over fifty years earlier. As soon as he found the ticket he sent the amount due, with a letter of apology. This shows remarkable integrity, but why should he have felt the need to do this? Nobody else knew what had happened and he was no longer in danger of being prosecuted, yet he felt it wrong to let it slide. Why? Why and how do we become aware of moral issues? The straightforward answer is that our moral awareness is triggered by the conscience, a mysterious moral monitor that pokes its nose into every nook and cranny of our lives, from the bedroom to the boardroom and from the way we spend our money to the way we use our time.

Conscience is more than instinct or desire. There are times when we have an instinct or desire to do something, but conscience tells us that we should not; and there are times when we have an instinct or desire not to do something, but conscience tells us that we should. Not every instinct or desire is in itself always right, but morality is, and the conscience not only points us to a moral law, but tells us in no uncertain terms that we ought to obey it. Linking the two together, Phillip Johnson says of the moral law, 'It is the bedrock moral understanding that we can't *not* know, however hard we try to evade that knowledge, because our consciences bear witness to it.'

Although it has no power to enforce our obedience, conscience wriggles its way into our thinking whenever we face moral choices. Even people who deny the existence of objective moral values agree that there is personal moral obligation, that to obey one's conscience is right and to disobey it is wrong. But what is the source of its authority? How does it relate to moral law? Vast as those questions are, the answer must come from one of only four possibilities.

## From atoms to ethics?

The first possibility is that our sense of morality comes from nature, that somehow or other it found its way into our genes over a long process of evolution. The claim is that a random mechanical process has tricked us into believing in a non-existent moral code, as obedience to it is the only means of our survival! Yet this collides head on with both logic and common sense. Materialist William Provine exposes the weakness of this case while endorsing an atheistic world view: 'Evolution teaches us virtually nothing about morality ... We humans are just on our own. We're put here by a process that doesn't care about us and we have to figure out for ourselves how to behave with each other.'

The idea that morals and ethics are the products of nature raises some hugely awkward questions. If the universe is nothing more than matter, energy, time and chance, how can these produce concepts of right and wrong? Can protons or neutrons nudge us in the right direction? How can the natural world, or the laws of nature, hold us responsible for our behaviour? Do we have any moral obligation to the laws of nature? Moral behaviour often involves the making and keeping of promises—but anybody known to make moral promises to anything in nature or to the laws of nature would hardly get high marks for common sense!

Newspaper columnist Martyn Harris was dying of cancer when he wrote, 'In a universe without God ... the only imperative to behave well is the knowledge that it is more dignified than to behave badly. It is better to live than not to live, and in deciding to live we make ethical creatures of ourselves.' It is difficult to see how 'deciding to live' makes us 'ethical'. Others have a very different response to the idea that we are nothing more than the random results of evolutionary development. The serial killer Geoffrey Dahmer murdered seventeen men between 1978 and 1991 (and ate body parts of some of them). Asked in prison why he did what he did he replied, 'Because I believed I came from slime through evolution, and that I was free to do anything I chose to do as long as I could get away with it.'

No sane person would suggest that all evolutionists are murderers or cannibals, but Dahmer's testimony shows that evolutionism paves the way for even the worst of depravity. If we are nothing more than bags of biological bits and pieces we have no moral obligations to anything—not even to other such bags! Scientist Rodney Holder gets to the heart of the matter when he says, 'If we are nothing but atoms and molecules organized in a particular way through the chance processes of evolution, then love, beauty, good and evil, free will, reason itself, indeed, all that makes us human and raises us above the rest of the created order, lose their objectivity. Why should I love my neighbour, or go out of my way to help him? Rather, why should I not get everything I can for myself, trampling on whoever gets in my way?' Not surprisingly, even the arch-atheist Richard Dawkins, while claiming to have 'a strongly developed sense of good', was forced to admit that 'As a biologist I haven't a very well worked-out story where that comes from,' and to concede that 'Universal love and the welfare of the species are concepts that simply do not make evolutionary sense.'

In trying to find a basis for behaviour, nature is not the answer, as it is impossible to jump from atoms to ethics and from molecules to morality. C. S. Lewis put it like this: 'If we are to make moral judgements (and whatever we say we shall in fact continue to do so) then we must believe that the conscience is not a product of Nature. It can be valid only if it is an offshoot of some absolute moral wisdom, a moral

13

wisdom which exists absolutely "on its own" and is not a product of non-moral, non-rational Nature.'

### Follow Frank?

Frank Sinatra, who died in 1998, was an American icon with a worldwide reputation for his voice and style, and BBC's Radio 2 even named him 'the greatest voice of the twentieth century'. All his obituaries drew attention to his best-known song, which began with these words:

> And now, the end is near,
> And so I face the final curtain.
> My friend, I'll say it clear,
> I'll state my case, of which I'm certain.
> I've lived a life that's full,
> I've travelled each and ev'ry highway
> And more, much more than this,
> I did it my way.

The last five words not only reflect Sinatra's general lifestyle, they also chime with much of today's thinking. On BBC Radio's *Desert Island Discs* 'My Way' was eventually banned because so many people wanted to have it played, reflecting the popular belief that 'my way' is the right way and individuals do not need to justify themselves or answer to anyone.

This is pure postmodernism, which sees reality as a series of unrelated fragments in which neither history nor literature can tell us anything. 'Meaning' is something created by the person who reads the book, watches the film, speaks the language, or lives the life.

Postmodernism is hugely popular (even among those who have never heard the word!) for one fundamental reason—it airbrushes God out of the picture. Nobody made this clearer than one of its most powerful advocates, the philosopher Jacques Derrida, who said that when applied to literature it was 'the death of God in writing'. Postmodernism spawns two closely related ideas, relativism and subjectivism. Simply stated, relativism says that there are no objective standards; as one writer put it, 'There is one thing a professor can be certain of. Almost every student entering the university believes, or says he believes, that truth is relative.' Yet relativism disintegrates as soon as we try to examine its implications. Roger Scruton points out, 'A writer who says that there are no truths, or that all truth is "merely negative", is asking you not to believe him. So don't.'

One brand of relativism says that morality developed over the course of time as a kind of social contract aimed at achieving the greatest good for the greatest number of people, but history teems with examples of rulers, politicians, scientists and others who have done horrific things in the name of this principle. Hitler would have signed up to the idea in a heartbeat. His elimination of over six million Jews, gypsies, blacks and other 'inferiors' in the infamous Holocaust was motivated by his determination to 'free Germany from the stupid and degrading fallacies of morality' and to develop a superior race, where the greatest number of the greatest good would be guaranteed. The terrorists who killed nearly 3,000 people in the despicable attack on the United States on 11 September 2001 were convinced not only that as martyrs they would gain a prominent place in paradise, but that they were serving a cause that would eventually benefit all mankind.

Subjectivism takes things a logical step further and says that, in the absence of objective standards, every individual is capable of setting valid ethical norms. But if every individual is justified in following his or her feelings in deciding issues of morality, nobody is under any moral obligation to anyone else.

Taken to its logical conclusion, subjectivism puts moral choices on a par with selecting items from a restaurant menu: Steak or salmon? Carrots or cauliflower? Wine or water? In claiming, 'The moral principles that govern our behaviour are rooted in habit and custom, feeling and fashion,' Paul Kurtz maintains that this is the case, but it is not difficult to show that privatizing ethics in this way is a recipe for social chaos. If morality is completely subjective, nobody can condemn what anybody else does, as even something considered grossly immoral by everybody else might be considered moral by the person concerned.

Ernest Hemingway once wrote, 'What is moral is what you feel good after, and what is immoral is what you feel bad after,' but does this hold good after gang rape, or when a young thug mugs an old lady in the street and steals the money in her purse to fuel his drug habit? No doubt the attackers feel good afterwards, but do their feelings sanctify their actions? Can we settle for saying that the attacks were right for the attackers but not for the victims? In the winter of 2005–6 a man broke into a house in the north of England, snatched a six-year-old girl from her bath and raped her before leaving her lying naked near her home when the temperature was only a few degrees above freezing. Within a short space of time media headlines on this case were shared by those telling of a three-year-old girl abducted, raped and found in a crashed car miles away from her home. Could anyone argue that what these attackers did was not relatively but *absolutely* wrong? And if these actions were absolutely wrong, where does this leave the argument that there are no moral absolutes? The person who denies moral absolutes has both feet firmly planted in mid-air. In words attributed to Fyodor Dostoevsky, 'Without God, everything is permitted.'

## Go with the flow?

Another idea that has widespread support goes under the name of multiculturalism. Underneath its wrapping, this says that nothing is outside the scope of culture, which pervades everything that human beings think, do, create and believe, so that religious claims, philosophical models and even scientific movements are all seen as 'social constructs'. As far as ethical principles are concerned, these are said to be determined by contemporary culture, with no superior law that overrides them.

Gordon Stein, once introduced as 'one of America's foremost scholars of atheism', spells out what this means: 'People's moral values are an accommodation they have made with their particular environment and have taught their children. It is a survival mechanism

… Evil is by definition in an atheist's universe that which decreases the happiness of people. That thing is evil which causes more people to be unhappy. How do we know this? Well, we don't know it. It's a consensus, just like morality in general is a consensus.'

We can easily list four reasons why tying morality to culture or a consensus is a non-starter.

Firstly, when considering moral issues, how can we be sure that public opinion is any better than private opinion? Does quantity guarantee quality? Can we really separate right from wrong by a show of hands? Why should a collection of individuals have any moral authority over a single person who fails to agree with their conclusions?

Secondly, if culture calls the tune, how can we claim that some are morally superior to others? If moral law reflects the view of the majority, or the strongest group, in a given society, what do we say when another society disagrees on details? How can there be a cultural basis for choosing between cultures? As one writer exposes and explains the problem: 'If a law is simply relative to culture, then, of course, it is impossible for one culture to judge another; each has its own law and each law is justified by the public opinion of its own people. But when the crunch comes we know that this view of law is wrong. At the Nuremberg trials the Nazis charged with war crimes said that they had simply been carrying out the orders and laws of the government of Germany. But this rationale was seen to be false. The Nuremberg trials were based on the concept that there is a higher law by which the laws of Nazi Germany could be tested.'

Thirdly, what do we say when a society's views on moral issues undergo a radical change? The previous point provides us with a perfect example, as the present German government utterly rejects the principles followed by the leadership of Nazi Germany. Is there a purely cultural reason why we can commend one and condemn the other?

Fourthly, some of the most honoured people in history are those who have rejected the culture of their times and fought tooth and nail against certain practices until radical changes were made. In the nineteenth century alone, William Wilberforce's campaign against slavery, Elizabeth Fry's pioneering of prison reform and the Earl of Shaftesbury's efforts on behalf of the working classes and the mentally ill were examples of those who refused to 'go with the flow' and overthrew practices that had been acceptable for centuries.

Writing as 'an agnostic Jew with no religious axe to grind', Janet Daley hit the nail on the head when she told her *Daily Telegraph* readers, 'It is a fundamental logical error to think that you can choose between cultures when a given culture, with its explicit moral programme, is the only equipment we have for making social choices. *If everyone is right then no one is.*'

## The alternative

So far, we have looked at three theoretically possible sources of Kant's 'moral law within'—nature, personal choice and the prevailing culture. These all fit into a world view that eliminates God, but none fits into what we know about moral law. Those who reject God can certainly do things they would claim to be 'good', *but they can offer no logical explanation as to why these actions can be described in this way*. Why is honesty better than dishonesty, humility better than pride, purity better than impurity, or love better than hatred?

We have already touched on the stock answer given by humanists and others who think like them, which is that morality is a matter of self-preservation and that we can determine what is 'good' on the basis of what promotes the greatest good of the greatest number of people. But this argument flies in the face of common sense and experience; we often exercise judgements on moral issues that have no direct bearing on our self-preservation or on the well-being of other people. In the absence of absolute values there is no basis on which we can make moral judgements about anything or anyone.

We have now seen that a solid basis for moral values must be rooted in something other than nature, personal preference or culture. This leaves us with only one other alternative, one basis on which moral judgements can be made—and several things must be true about it.

Firstly, it must be *transcendent*. We should hardly need to argue this point, but if the distinction between good and evil is radical and real and there is no natural basis for defining it, there must be a supernatural one, completely unaffected by human assessments, which can so easily be tainted by self-interest or some other questionable motive. C. S. Lewis made the point brilliantly in recalling the time when he was an atheist: 'My argument against God was that the universe seemed so cruel and unjust. But how had I got this idea of *just and unjust*? A man does not call a line crooked unless he has some idea of a straight line. What was I comparing the universe with when I called it unjust? If the whole show was bad and senseless from A to Z, so to speak, why did I, who was supposed to be part of the show, find myself in such violent reaction against it? ... Thus in the very act of trying to prove that God did not exist—in other words, that the whole of reality was senseless—I was forced to assume that one part of reality—namely my idea of justice— was full of sense. Consequently atheism turns out to be too simple. If the universe has no meaning, we should never have found out that it has no meaning.'

Secondly, it must *be perfect*, or it would be unable to pass infallible judgement on moral issues. I have a heart condition that calls for regular check-ups, when the meticulous ECG readings taken depend on an absolute scale of reference given by the equipment the doctor is using. On my last visit he had new equipment, but its impressive technology would have been useless without an absolute standard of reference.

Thirdly, it must be *unchanging*, not affected in any way by swings in popular conceptions of moral issues. It would be impossible to play the moral game if the goalposts kept being moved!

These three requirements seem clear and obvious, but there is another: it must be *personal*. Conscience tells us that there are things we ought to do and things we ought not to do. The word 'ought' is a contraction of 'owe it' and speaks of moral obligation. Yet moral obligations involve personal relationships. To illustrate what I mean, we are all subject to the law of gravity, but we have no moral obligation to obey it. Absolute standards call for absolute obligations and for the reasons we have just seen absolute obligations must relate to a reality that is transcendent, perfect, unchanging and personal.

## Four out of four

This may suggest that finding a sound basis for 'the moral law within' is very difficult—but the God revealed in the Bible meets all four of the necessary requirements.

### He is transcendent

The opening words in the Bible make this crystal clear: 'In the beginning God created the heavens and the earth' (Genesis 1:1). This tells us that God is the uncreated Creator of all reality outside of himself—from angels to atoms, from elephants to energy, from titanium to time, from dolphins to DNA, from stars to the space in which he placed them—and that he did so out of nothing. As the Bible puts it, 'By faith we understand that the universe was created by the word of God, so that what is seen was not made out of things that are visible' (Hebrews 11:3). God is distinct and separate from the entire universe and from everything in it, and can no more be confined to space than he can be measured by time. He is the absolute and all else is relative. The Bible reduces all of these truths to just five words in saying that he is 'exalted as head above all' (1 Chronicles 29:11).

### He is perfect
God's perfection is stamped all over Scripture. He is the 'perfection of beauty' (Psalm 50:2); 'his way is perfect' (2 Samuel 22:31); 'his work is perfect' (Deuteronomy 32:4); he is 'perfect in knowledge' (Job 36:4) and 'the law of the LORD is perfect' (Psalm 19:7). God has no moral flaws, weaknesses, imperfections or shortcomings. He has what one scholar has called 'total and unique moral majesty' and defines good and evil *by what he is.* Everything that clashes with God's perfection is therefore evil and wrong. Yet God goes far beyond moral perfection. The Bible speaks of 'the splendour of (his) holiness' (1 Chronicles 16:29) and of his 'glorious splendour' (Psalm 145:5). As C. S. Lewis says, 'A man can no more diminish God's glory than a lunatic can put out the sun by scribbling "darkness" on the walls of his cell.'

### He is unchanging
In the Bible's words, he 'does not change like shifting shadows' (James 1:17 NIV). He alone can truthfully say, 'I the LORD do not change' (Malachi 3:6). Everything in nature is in a constant state of flux, while as human beings we are not only getting older by the minute, but constantly revising our options and opinions, preferences and positions. By dazzling contrast, God is utterly reliable and unchangeably stable in all he thinks, says and does.

### He is personal

When atheist Peter Atkins mocked theists as believing in 'this unknown thing up there that we have to spend our time kow-towing to', he betrayed his abysmal ignorance of what the Bible says. Far from defining God as cosmic dust, atmospheric energy or some kind of 'higher power' or influence, the Bible tells us that he is dynamically alive. He thinks, cares, gives, and makes (and keeps) promises. He is described as being 'good' (Psalm 25:8), 'faithful' (Deuteronomy 7:9), 'compassionate and gracious' (Psalm 103:8), 'merciful and forgiving' (Daniel 9:9) and 'abounding in love' (Joel 2:13)—characteristics that could never apply to Peter Atkins's caricature. Peter Moore is not exaggerating when he writes, 'The ultimate fact about the universe is a personal God.' Francis Collins, former Director of the National Human Genome Research Institute, agrees: 'The moral law, which defies scientific explanation, is exactly what one might expect to find if one were searching for the existence of a personal God who sought relationship with mankind.'

Trying to live a consciously moral life while denying the existence of God is like driving a car with your eyes closed; there is no way of telling in which direction you are going. With God at the centre of your world view, the place and purpose of conscience become clear. Even those who deny God's existence have his law 'written on their hearts' (Romans 2:15). Conscience is God's fingerprint on the human heart, giving each one of us an inbuilt moral awareness.

But the Bible goes even further and speaks of 'that day when ... God judges the secrets of men' (Romans 2:16).

There is an ancient public policy in legal matters that says ignorance of the law is no excuse. This holds that a person who is unaware of a law may not escape liability for breaking that law merely because he or she was unaware of its content. The Bible says much the same thing in stating that breaking God's law makes the person concerned guilty and answerable to God on the day of final judgement, regardless of how much or little the individual in question may know of what the law of God says. Those who would claim that this is unfair are forgetting that whenever they pass judgement on their own behaviour, or on the behaviour of others, they are confirming that both parties are under the authority of a transcendent moral code. As atheist and scholar Richard Taylor freely admits, 'The concept of moral obligation [is] unintelligible apart from the idea of God. The words remain but their meaning is gone.'

## The bigger question

There is a sense in which the question, 'Can we be good without God?' is a non-starter, because without a transcendent, perfect, unchanging and personal basis for morality we have no way of defining right or wrong—and only God has all of those qualities. But accepting God as the ultimate reference point for determining moral absolutes raises a question that surely exercises anybody who thinks seriously about morality: 'Can we be good enough for God without

God?' Studying two cases recorded in the Bible will give us a clear answer to the question.

## Case study 1

This comes in the form of a parable told by Jesus to some people 'who trusted in themselves that they were righteous, and treated others with contempt' (Luke 18:9). This is how it reads:

> Two men went up into the temple to pray, one a Pharisee and the other a tax collector. The Pharisee, standing by himself, prayed thus:'God, I thank you that I am not like other men, extortioners, unjust, adulterers, or even like this tax collector. I fast twice a week; I give tithes of all that I get.' But the tax collector, standing far off, would not even lift up his eyes to heaven, but beat his breast, saying, 'God, be merciful to me, a sinner! ' I tell you, this man went down to his house justified, rather than the other. For everyone who exalts himself will be humbled, but the one who humbles himself will be exalted
>
> (Luke 18:10–14).

The great temple in Jerusalem was the focal point of the nation's religion and here were two men who were going there to pray, to seek God's face and to know his blessing on their lives.

The first was a *Pharisee*. Of all the Jewish sects, the Pharisees were the most radical. God's law had been handed down to the Jewish nation from the days of Moses, but there were many who sat rather loosely to it. The Pharisees, a religious party formed between

Old Testament and New Testament times, reacted strongly to this approach and aimed at meticulous obedience not merely to the law of God in general, but also to a mass of rules and regulations that had been imposed on it by a succession of scholars. In fact, the Pharisees often attached more importance to these than to the law itself and came to believe that strict obedience to them would bring about the coming of the Messiah (the 'anointed one') and guarantee their own acceptance into the kingdom of God. Though their numbers included men of the highest character and integrity, the New Testament generally gives them a very bad press, frequently condemning them for their self-righteousness and hypocrisy.

The second was a *tax collector*. In modern society tax officials can be models of integrity, but it seems that this man was not in that league. Those employed by the occupying Romans were easily able to fiddle the books and keep some of the money back for themselves. Jewish tax collectors were already considered traitors by their fellow Jews and their reputation for dishonesty added to their shame and made them deeply hated as a group. They were so despised that the New Testament often lumps them together with other undesirables in the phrase 'tax collectors and "sinners"' (e.g. Matthew 9:11). If they had offered a gift to their local synagogue it would have been refused.

First to pray was the Pharisee, who prayed about himself: "God, I thank you…" Thanking God sounds like a fine beginning, but it is ruined by the fact that what follows is an exercise in self-congratulation, in which God never gets another mention. 'I am not like other men,' tells us that he thought that he was a cut above everybody else—and he goes on to look down on three groups in particular—'extortioners', 'unjust' and 'adulterers'.

'Extortioners' is based on the Greek word for the grappling iron that pirates would use to board a ship and it described greedy extortionists, prepared to do anything to feather their own nests.

'Unjust' were people dishonest in their dealings with others. It is said that the Greek cynic Diogenes once walked through the streets of Athens carrying a lighted candle in broad daylight. When someone asked him what he was doing he replied, 'I am looking for an honest man.' Little has changed: in politics, industry, business, sport and family relationships, who can claim to be completely honest in their words and actions?

The meaning of 'adulterers' is perfectly straightforward. In pagan society at least, attitudes towards sexual behaviour were as loose as they are in similar settings today, but the Pharisees took a very different view and judged adultery to be a degrading and disgusting sin. The Pharisee claimed that he was neither greedy, dishonest nor immoral (and we have no reason to question his claim). Catching sight of the other man at the temple, he proudly added the footnote that he was 'not even like this tax collector', whose reputation stank.

The Pharisee then ramped up his case even further by reminding God of two specific ways in which he believed he merited reward: 'I fast twice a week and give a tenth of all I get.' Fasting (in the sense of going without food for a certain time) is not specifically commanded in Old Testament law, though Jews commonly fasted on *Yom Kippur* (the Day of Atonement), which was an annual time of spiritual self-examination. Later, fasting was observed up to four times a year, but the Pharisee was not content with this and went without food twice a week. Tithing (consecrating one-tenth of one's major crops and cattle to God) was laid down in Old Testament law (e.g. Leviticus 27:30–32), but the Pharisee boasted that he went further and set aside for God's service ten per cent of his entire income.

## The fatal flaw

Now comes the crunch: this man left the temple rejected by God and condemned! The key to understanding this is to remember that Jesus told the story to those who were confident of their own righteousness. The Pharisee went to the temple to pray, but his 'prayer' consisted of nothing more than elaborately blowing his own trumpet by reciting his virtues and assuming that they would be sufficient to be accepted by God. But he was making a tragic and fundamental mistake, as the Bible makes it crystal clear that nobody is made right with God 'by works of the law' (Galatians 2:16) and lays down four clear reasons why this is the case.

Firstly, 'the law is spiritual' (Romans 7:14). It reaches deeper than our words and actions; it judges our thoughts, motives and desires. God requires truth 'in the inward being' (Psalm 51:6), and not merely in the things others can see and hear. Our words and actions may seem fine, but would we be just as happy for people to see what goes on in our hearts and minds?

Secondly, 'the law of the LORD is perfect' (Psalm 19:7) and the person who aims to get right with God by keeping his commandments would need to keep every one of them. The required standard is perfection and anything short of this means failure—and punishment.

Thirdly, this means that even one sin is enough to condemn a person. We have not all sinned in the same way, or to the same extent, or with the same understanding of what we were doing, but 'All have sinned and fall short of the glory of God' (Romans 3:23), and even one sin would be sufficient to condemn us.

Fourthly, God's law was not given to make us right with God, but to show us that we were not! In the Bible's own words, 'through the law comes knowledge of sin' (Romans 3:20). The law of God can diagnose sin, but not deliver anyone from it. It can reveal sin, but not remedy it. It can show you that you are away from God, but not bring you any nearer to him. The Pharisee failed to grasp any of these four tremendous truths. Are you making the same mistake?

Now it is the tax collector's turn to pray, but even before he says a word we can tell that his whole attitude is very different from that of the Pharisee. He was 'stating far off'—still within the temple precincts, but not at a central point where he would be noticed by other worshippers. He would not even look up to heaven, but bowed his head in recognition that he was coming before a holy God, not putting on an outward show to impress any onlookers. Finally, he 'beat his breast'. The tense of the verb here means that the tax collector *kept on* beating his breast, a sign of deep sorrow, regret and despair. Then came his prayer: 'God, be merciful to me, a sinner.' This English translation misses the important point that the original words literally mean, 'God, have mercy on me, *the* sinner.' Both men believed they were in a class of their own, but for very different reasons. Whereas the Pharisee boasted that he was *better* than everybody else, the tax collector claimed that he was *worse* than anybody else. He saw himself as being guilty, lost and helpless, without a shred of goodness that would commend him to God and deserving only of his anger and judgement.

In this state he prays for just one thing, but it was the thing he needed above all else—God's mercy. He cried out for God to remove his righteous anger from him, so that he could be forgiven, restored and accepted by God, but he realized that this could only come about if he cast himself completely on God's mercy. His prayer is virtually a précis of one offered by Israel's King David centuries earlier:

> Have mercy on me, O God,
> according to your steadfast love;
> according to your abundant mercy
> blot out my transgressions.
> Wash me thoroughly from my iniquity,
> and cleanse me from my sin!
> For I know my transgressions,
> and my sin is ever before me …

Create in me a clean heart, O God

(Psalm 51:1–3,10).

If the tax collector's prayer was radically different from that of the Pharisee, so was its outcome, as Jesus said that 'This man went down to his house justified, rather than the other.' The Pharisee brought before God a news bulletin of his own achievements; the tax collector brought a broken heart. The Pharisee blew his own trumpet; the tax collector beat his own breast— and the God who 'opposes the proud but gives grace to the humble' (James 4:6) responded accordingly. The tax collector left the temple justified before God, his prayer answered, his sins forgiven and at peace with God. The Pharisee left the temple just as he had entered it, rejected and condemned. The whole story powerfully illustrates the biblical truth that 'Whoever exalts himself will be humbled, and whoever humbles himself will be exalted' (Matthew 23:12). It also sheds light on the answer to the question, 'Can we be good enough for God without God?' We will come back to this when we have examined another case.

## Case study 2

The second case study is of a religious extremist by the name of Saul. Piecing together his background from the fragments of evidence available, we know that he was born in Tarsus, now a Turkish city on the Mediterranean. Located where several important trade routes met, it was an important urban centre with a sizeable Jewish community and is said to have rivalled Athens and Alexandria in its passion for education and philosophy. It was also a hotbed of religious ideas and host to what has been called 'a dizzying array of gods and faiths'.

Although he was a 'tentmaker' by trade (Acts 18:3), we also know that Saul's higher education included some time in Jerusalem where, as a student of Gamaliel, a distinguished doctor of Jewish law, he was thoroughly trained 'according to the strict manner of the law of our fathers' (Acts 22:3). Later in life this outstanding scholar added the Latin name 'Paul' to his original Hebrew name 'Saul', and from then on 'Paul' is the name by which he was known.

In words written to the earliest Christian church at Philippi, in the north-eastern corner of Greece, he provides us with our second case study, beginning with these words:

> If anyone else thinks he has reason for confidence in the flesh, I have more: circumcised on the eighth day, of the people of Israel, of the tribe of Benjamin, a Hebrew of Hebrews; as to the law, a Pharisee; as to zeal, a persecutor of the church; as to righteousness, under the law blameless
>
> (Philippians 3:4–6).

He is obviously referring to people who went along with the popular notion that they could get right with God by their own religious status or efforts. They put 'confidence in the flesh' and believed that by adding their moral and spiritual actions to their religious pedigree they could be sure that God would accept them and that at the end of life they would be guaranteed a place in heaven.

Paul tackles their arrogance head-on and begins by saying that whatever reason they might have for making such a claim he had more, and then backs this up by listing seven major factors in which he had once trusted. To make them flow a little more easily into our modern way of thinking I will change the order a little.

*1. 'Of the people of Israel.'* Paul's first thrust is to say that he was born a Jew. This was a huge 'plus' in the minds of the people to whom he was writing. In religious terms, the Jews considered themselves a race apart, with the rest of the world's population lumped together as 'Gentiles' or 'Greeks' (even those with no Greek connection). What marked the Jews off from the rest of mankind in the ancient world was that they alone believed in one God. The Romans and the Greeks each had a pantheon of deities, while other nations and tribes worshipped countless idols they had invented. Paul rejected all of this idolatry and heathenism and made it clear that he was of pure Israelite descent.

*2. 'Of the tribe of Benjamin.'* Having claimed national advantage, Paul now refers to his ancestral advantage. After the death of King Solomon in 930 BC, a civil war divided the 'united kingdom' of the Jewish people into ten northern tribes and two southern tribes. The northern tribes, commonly called 'Israel', were ruled by a succession of nineteen kings, almost all of whom led Israel deeper into instability, immorality and idolatry until eventually it was wiped off the map for ever. The two southern tribes, Judah and Benjamin (usually together called Judah), had a mixture of kings, some good and some bad, and lasted 140 years longer than Israel before being invaded by the Babylonians, under King Nebuchadnezzar. Jerusalem was flattened, Solomon's temple, the great centre of the nation's religion, was burned to the ground and the cream of the population was deported to Babylonia. But the exile lasted only about seventy years and in a remarkable set of circumstances the people of Judah were allowed to return home, rebuild Jerusalem, restore the temple and reconstitute the religious structure of the nation. This piece of history may seem remote to us today, but it is important to bear it in mind because of Paul's claim to come from the tribe of Benjamin, one of only two that remained faithful to God during over 300 years of turmoil.

*3. 'Circumcised on the eighth day.'* This may seem irrelevant to non-Jews reading these words now, but in Paul's day it was hugely significant. God ordained circumcision upon Abraham, the ancestor and founder of the entire Jewish nation, as a token of the covenant into which they had entered with him. It was a condition of a Jewish male's nationality; there are places in the Bible where those who do not worship the true God are referred to as 'the uncircumcised' (e.g. Ezekiel 31:18). Male converts to Judaism were circumcised at the time of their conversion, but Paul was no latecomer to the Jewish faith. He could point to his being a pure-blooded Jew in having been circumcised when he was eight days old, exactly as laid down in the original covenant with Abraham (Genesis 17:9–12).

*4. 'A Hebrew of Hebrews.'* Paul now reaches even further back to establish his religious credentials and says that he was 'a Hebrew of Hebrews'. He was not a converted outsider, but had been born into a Hebrew (Jewish) family, his zealously religious parents having kept their Jewish faith, language and customs even though living in a foreign country. This was the foundation stone of these impressive inherited credentials. Now he turns to what he had done to build on their foundation.

5. *'As to the law, a Pharisee.'* Elsewhere, Paul underlines this by saying that he was not only a Pharisee but 'the son of a Pharisee' (Acts 23:6). He prided himself on belonging to what he called 'the strictest sect of our religion' (Acts 26:5) and on being 'extremely zealous for the traditions of my fathers' (Galatians 1:14). As we saw in our first case study, the Pharisees set great store by a mass of rules and regulations imposed on the Old Testament law of God and believed that obedience to these was their passport to the kingdom of heaven. Paul was steeped in this idea, which dominated his thinking.

6. *'As to righteousness, under the law blameless.'* This tells us that Paul put his thinking into practice. He was so meticulous in his application of the legalistic framework that scholars had imposed on God's law that he challenged anyone to fault him. But he went even further.

7. *'As to zeal, a persecutor of the church.'* 'The church' was the Christian church, whose founder, Jesus, had angrily denounced the Pharisees for their self-righteousness and taught that getting right with God was dependent on God's grace, and not on man's

effort. This infuriated the Pharisees, and Paul was so convinced that toeing the law's line was the *only* way to get right with God that he went on a search-and-destroy mission against those who thought otherwise. We find him 'breathing out murderous threats' (Acts 9:1) against the early church, getting warrants from the religious authorities so that if he found any Christians in and around synagogues, 'whether men or women, he might take them as prisoners to Jerusalem' (Acts 9:2). Elsewhere he says that he 'persecuted the followers of this Way [the Christian church] to their death' (Acts 22:4). He 'went from one synagogue to another to have them punished,' 'tried to force them to blaspheme' and in his 'obsession against them ... even went to foreign cities to persecute them' (Acts 26:11). When Stephen, the first Christian martyr, was executed by stoning, 'Saul was there, giving approval to his death' (Acts 8:1).

With this evidence on the table we can easily see why Paul would have felt justified in calling himself an earnest, obedient servant of God, rightly doing everything he could to root out a blasphemous sect that he believed was undermining the law of God laid down in the Old Testament.

## Profit and loss

Now watch this! After laying out these seven reasons, four inherited and three earned, why he could outrank anybody who claimed that they had 'confidence in the flesh', Paul suddenly turns his whole testimony on its head:

> But whatever gain I had, I counted as loss for the sake of Christ ... and count them as rubbish, in

order that I may gain Christ and be found in him, not having a righteousness of my own that comes from the law, but that which comes through faith in Christ, the righteousness from God that depends on faith (Philippians 3:7–9, ESV).

In using the words 'gain' and 'loss' Paul is writing as if he were a businessman or accountant, totalling up entries in the ledger of his life. The original word translated 'gain' in the opening phrase is plural and is a blanket term covering all the things on which he had previously set such store. Yet as soon as he had come to faith in Christ he had realized that, far from being of any benefit to him in terms of his relationship with God, they could all be labelled 'loss'. This had not been a starry-eyed fantasy, an emotional outburst, or a sudden rush of religious blood to the head, but a powerful, emphatic conviction. This brilliant thinker, steeped from birth in religious ideas that saw getting right with God as a combination of ancestry and effort, had his thinking revolutionized as soon as he came into a living relationship with Christ.

Now, as a maturing Christian, he had come to see that the things he had once counted as gains were not merely a complete 'loss' but 'rubbish'. The original Greek word, *skubalon*, literally means 'something thrown to the dogs'. Elsewhere in the literature of the time it is used of dregs, refuse, things that are worthless, the filth of the mind, and even of dung. This is startling language! Paul looks back on his racial, ancestral and ecclesiastical privileges and on a lifetime of dedication to the outward observance of every dot and comma of the law of Moses, and now says that in terms of making him right with God these things have no more merit than manure!

This may sound irrational and ridiculous, but abandoning trust in human privilege or effort is one of the bedrock biblical requirements of getting right with God. One of the Old Testament prophets put it just as bluntly as Paul when he wrote, 'All of us have become like one who is unclean, and all our righteous acts are like filthy rags' (Isaiah 64:6, NIV). The words 'filthy rags' translate a Hebrew phrase for clothing stained by a woman's menstrual blood, and the prophet is saying that in terms of making us right with God even the best things we do—'our righteous acts'—are not only powerless but polluted.

Three New Testament passages develop this with devastating logic. The first says, 'For whoever keeps the whole law but fails in one point has become accountable for all of it. . . If you do not commit adultery but do murder, you have become a transgressor of the law' (James 2:10–11). We dare not miss the message here! It is not saying that the person who commits one particular sin is to be held guilty of committing every other sin, nor is it saying that to break one part of the law of God is to break every part of it. What it is saying is that *God's law is an entity and that even one sin results in the law as a whole being broken*. It is not like an examination paper that requires only six questions out of ten to be attempted. Nor is it like a pile of stones, from which one can be removed without any significant difference to the size of the pile. Instead, it is like a pane of glass—one crack and the entire pane is broken. We could use any number of other illustrations to make the same point: one puncture and the whole tyre is flat; one severed link and the whole chain is broken; one leak and the boat is sunk. The Bible can have no takers when it asks, 'Who can say, "I have made my heart pure; I am clean from my sin"' (Proverbs 20:9).

In the second passage, Paul confirms this in the most emphatic way possible by endorsing the Old Testament's teaching: 'None is righteous, no, not one … no one does good, not even one' (Romans 3:10, 12). Theologians call this the doctrine of total depravity. This does not mean that every thought, word and action of every person is as evil as it is possible to be, but it does mean that even the best of our thoughts, words and actions are affected to some extent by our inherent sinfulness.

In the third passage, Paul adds the obvious point that the person who tries to justify himself by religious observance (he had circumcision in mind at the time) is therefore doomed to failure because he is 'obligated to keep *the whole law*' (Galatians 5:3, emphasis added). Earlier in the same letter he adapted an Old Testament statement and wrote, 'All who rely on observing the law are under a curse, for it is written: "For all who rely on works of the law are under a curse; for it is written, "Cursed be everyone who does not abide by all things written in the Book of the Law, and do them." Now it is evident that no one is justified before God by the law' (Galatians 3:10–11). This was in no way downgrading the law, but pointing out that it had been given not as some kind of examination paper (as the only pass mark acceptable to God would be 100%), but, in the first place, to show where we are going wrong—in other words to convince us that we are lawbreakers, guilty sinners in the sight of a holy God. The first step each of us needs to take in order to get right with God is to realize that left to ourselves we are in the wrong with God—and the law has been given to show us that this is the case.

## The downward spiral

So far, the story has gone from bad to worse, as we can see if we summarize and underline what we have discovered.

No rational person can deny that as human beings we have an innate sense that there is a radical difference between right and wrong. Trying to deny this is like playing games with dynamite.

This moral sense is triggered by the conscience, a moral monitor that judges our thoughts, words and actions.

We can find no consistent and dependable moral basis for conscience in nature, in ourselves or in culture.

God alone is the explanation for our moral sense, as without him we have no infallible way of differentiating between right and wrong.

The bigger question is, 'Can we be good enough for God without God?' and the answer is an emphatic 'No'. The Bible drives this home in the clearest possible way by saying that 'All have sinned and fall short of the glory of God' (Romans 3:23). It is important to notice that while 'sinned' is in the past tense, 'fall short' is in the present tense, indicating that this falling short is something constantly going on. Not only have we failed to live up to God's law (which is a reflection of his nature), but *we continue to do so every day of our lives.* One single statement in Scripture is sufficient to show that trying to dodge this verdict is pointless. When someone asked Jesus, 'Of all the commandments, which is the most important?' he replied, 'The most important one ... is this: ... Love the Lord your God with all your heart and with all your soul and with all your mind and with all your strength' (Mark 12:28–29 NIV). This brilliant summary of the first four of the Ten Commandments leaves each one of us 'guilty as charged' and to deny that this is the case adds to our guilt. Yet I have never attended the funeral of a 'bad' person! Time and again even someone who had had no obvious connection with spiritual things, let alone with organized religion, is spoken of in glowing terms: 'He never did anyone any harm'; 'She was kind to everyone'; 'He was honest and upright in everything he did', or 'She was a fine friend and neighbour.' Whitewashing the deceased may be of some comfort to mourners, but it hardly gives a completely honest picture.

No advantages we may have inherited by means of race or religion do anything to overcome, or even reduce, this moral deficit. Whatever our ancestry, background or upbringing, whatever religious rituals or ceremonies we may have performed (including those practised by the Christian church), they all leave us cut off from God.

Even the very best things we think, say or do are equally powerless. No amount of honesty, purity, humility, love or kindness can cancel out our sins.

To this dreadful downward spiral the Bible adds one final twist. It says that those who die in this state will be judged by God, who is 'perfect in knowledge' (Job 37:16), whose 'eyes are too pure to look on evil' (Habakkuk 1:13) and who has already determined that 'nothing impure will ever enter (heaven)' (Revelation 21:27). Those whose godless lives have reflected their rebellion against God's rule will be 'punished with everlasting destruction and shut out from the presence of the Lord and from the majesty of his power' (2 Thessalonians 1:9). To put it even more bluntly, they will be 'thrown into hell' (Matthew 5:29).

## The ultimate answer

The law of God, crystallized in the Ten Commandments, has been given to show us that, left to ourselves, we are all exposed to this appalling fate—but the Bible tells us that the law has another purpose. It pictures humankind not merely as lawbreakers but as prisoners, with the law of God as a prison officer, holding the guilty in custody so that they will always be conscious of their guilt and of their liability to punishment, yet at the same time pointing them to the only way in which their sin can be dealt with and their imprisonment ended. In the Bible's own words, 'Now before faith came, we were held captive under the law, imprisoned until the coming faith would be revealed. So then, the law was our guardian *until Christ came*, in order that we might be justified by faith' (Galatians 3:23).

The words I have emphasized are at the very heart of the Bible's message. The Old Testament includes large chunks of history, poetry and prophecy, yet all thirty-nine books are united in pointing not to a principle but to a person, the Messiah whom God promised to send to deliver his people. Some 400 years after the last Old Testament book had been written, Jesus of Nazareth was born and as soon as he came to public notice he began to demonstrate that he *was* the Messiah. The Greek equivalent of the Hebrew 'Messiah' is 'Christ', a word applied to Jesus over 500 times in the New Testament, either as a title or as part of a personal name, while his birthplace, lifestyle, character, power, influence, suffering, death—and resurrection—endorse the Bible's claim that beyond all question he was not only the true Messiah but 'the Son of the living God' (Matthew 16:16) who 'came into the world to save sinners' (1 Timothy 1:15). It has been calculated that Jesus fulfilled over 300 Messianic prophecies, something that makes sense only if we accept his own clear claim that 'The [Old Testament] Scriptures … testify about me' (John 5:39).

To understand how he saves sinners we need to focus not on his birth or life, but on his death, which occupies about one third of the Gospels, the closest we get to a biography of Jesus. The most significant thing he did was to die, which explains why the universal symbol of the Christian faith is not a reminder of his sinless character, his matchless teaching, or his stunning miracles, but a cross, the cruellest instrument of torture and execution known to the ancient world.

The link between sin and death is so strong that the Bible calls it 'the law of sin and death' (Romans 8:2). This law is as fixed and fundamental as the law of gravity. Death, physical and spiritual, is God's righteous punishment for sin. Before sin entered the world, death was impossible; ever since, it has been inevitable. But this seems to present a serious problem. As a genuine human being, Jesus was 'one who in every respect has been tempted as we are, yet without sin' (Hebrews 4:15). Then why did he die? The Bible's answer to that question is marvellous and momentous: 'Christ also suffered once for sins, the righteous for the unrighteous, that he might bring us to God' (1 Peter 3:18). Elsewhere it says that 'but God shows his love for us in that while we were still sinners, Christ died for us' (Romans 5:8).

Here is the amazing answer to the question, 'How can a righteous God ever wipe out anybody's sin and declare that person acceptable in his sight without bending the rules and compromising his own righteousness?' To look at it from another angle, how can God punish sin (as he must) yet declare a sinner free from guilt and its consequences? God's staggering solution to these otherwise impossible dilemmas was provided in the life and death of his Son, Jesus Christ. God's law demands that it be kept to perfection and that all who fail to do so must pay its penalty in full—and Jesus did both! His life was 'holy, blameless, pure, set apart from sinners' (Hebrews 7:26), yet in his death he paid in full sin's physical and spiritual penalty.

This was not some 'smoke-and-mirrors' arrangement between God the Father and God the Son. Instead, Jesus, God in human form, paid sin's debt in full; as someone has rightly said, 'He passed to the uttermost limit of sin's outworking.'

The reality of what Jesus accomplished in his death was certified three days later when he 'was declared to be the Son of God in power according to the Spirit of holiness by his resurrection from the dead' (Romans 1:4), an event based on such a mass of unshakeable evidence that 2,000 years later nobody has been able to make a single dent in the Bible's claim that 'Jesus died and rose again' (1 Thessalonians 4:14). Over 500 people saw him over the following six weeks before he ascended into heaven and millions since have testified to his living power in their lives.

### The turning point
One all-important question remains: how can anyone benefit from what Jesus accomplished in his life and death? How can the life and death of Jesus enable anyone to have their sins forgiven and to come into a living and eternal relationship with God? The issue is so urgent and personal I want to switch to writing in the second person singular, to write to *you* and not to an anonymous readership—and I also want to base the remainder of this booklet on an Old Testament statement that is powerfully relevant at this point: 'Those who cling to worthless idols forfeit the grace that could be theirs' (Jonah 2:8 NIV).

The first thing to notice is that there are people who miss out on 'grace that could be theirs' (we will examine this shortly) for one simple reason: they 'cling to worthless idols'. The *Oxford Dictionary of English* describes an idol as 'an image or representation of a god used as an object of worship' and the essential thing about an idol is that it is man-made. Idols obviously include the deities invented by civilizations such as the ancient Greek and Roman empires, as well as the millions of gods found in ancient religions from the East and elsewhere. But idols can also be *ideas*, notions that people have and to which they commit their lives. The idea that we earn our way into a right relationship with God, or at least contribute to it, is undoubtedly one of these.

We have already seen that this idea is baseless and bankrupt, but let me press this home to you. If, on the question of getting right with God, you are trusting in your background and claiming such things as, 'I was born in a Christian country' (there is no such place, by the way), or 'I was raised in a Christian home', you are clinging to a worthless idol. If you are looking to the fact that you were christened, dedicated, confirmed, baptized or received into church membership, you are clinging to a worthless idol. If you are trusting in the fact that you attend church occasionally (or even regularly) or that you support church causes by your giving of time or money, you are clinging to a worthless idol. If you are setting any store by the fact that you hold office in a church or other religious organization, or have a record of faithful service in charitable work aimed at helping those in need, you are clinging to a worthless idol. If you are banking on a claim that because your life is morally and spiritually better than that of many other people God will take your honesty, integrity, kindness and morality into account when determining your destiny, you are clinging to a worthless idol.

Millions of people make an equally tragic mistake by assuming that because 'God is love' (1 John 4:8) he will sweep all their failings under the carpet and receive them into heaven. But there is not a shred of biblical evidence to support this, whereas time and again there is the clearest warning that this will not happen. If everybody will be received into heaven regardless of their belief or behaviour, why did Jesus warn that unrepentant sinners would 'go away to eternal punishment'? (Matthew 25:46). If he was wrong, he must either have been ignorant (not knowing that everybody would go to heaven) or unethical (frightening people with terrifying threats he knew to be totally baseless). Universalism, the idea that God guarantees heaven for everyone, is nothing but a worthless idol.

Trying to get right with God by any of these means is like trying to heal a festering wound by covering it with a germ-ridden cloth. The first step you need to take is to turn away from trusting in any of them. You must abandon whatever confidence you are placing in any of them and recognize that they are utterly worthless as far as making you right with God is concerned; like the apostle Paul, you must 'consider them rubbish'. The Bible's word for doing this is *repentance* and Jesus made it clear that 'Unless you repent, you ... will ... perish' (Luke 13:3). To repent is to turn from sin—including the sin of trusting in anything other than Jesus Christ. It involves a change of mind, a change of heart and a change of will. Nothing less will do:

let the wicked forsake his way,
and the unrighteous man his thoughts;
let him return to the Lord, that he may have
compassion on him,
and to our God, for he will abundantly pardon
(Isaiah 55:7).

Notice the order of these words! You must forsake your sin before God will forgive it. There must be repentance *from* sin, not merely regret *for* it. Repentance is not real unless there is a genuine willingness to part with sin and to live in a way that is pleasing to God.

If the first step in becoming a true Christian is repentance, the second is *faith*. The words 'faith' and 'believing' are among the most frequently used about becoming a Christian, yet they are also among the most commonly misunderstood and misused. When the Bible commands you to 'believe' in Jesus Christ, or to have 'faith' in him, it means much more than to believe that he existed, or even to believe that he is the eternal Son of God who came into the world to save sinners. This is made clear by the fact that that an evil spirit once declared that Jesus is 'the Holy One of God' (Mark 1:24), a stunning confirmation of the Bible's claim that 'Even the demons believe ... and shudder' (James 2:19).

As with repentance, the faith you need must involve your mind, your heart and your will. It must involve your *mind,* in that you must accept that Jesus is exactly who he claimed to be. As he himself states, 'If you do not believe that I am the one I claim to be, you will … die in your sins' (John 8:24). Do you believe with your mind? Do you truly believe that his claim was true, that he is 'the true God' (1 John 5:20) and that he came into the world to save sinners like you?

It must involve your *heart.* The heart is the centre of your emotions, desires and affections, and the Bible says, 'It is with your heart that you believe and are justified' (Romans 10:10). Do you believe with your heart? Are you gripped with the truth your mind has grasped? Do you sense that Jesus died for *you?* Do you long to turn from the sins that caused his death and to trust him as your personal Saviour?

It must also involve your *will.* The faith that joins a person to Jesus Christ is an act of personal commitment, not merely a combination of knowledge and feelings. This aspect of faith is not so much believing *in* Jesus as believing *on* (or *upon*) him. It means flinging yourself upon him as fully as a drowning person would trust a lifeboat, a patient a surgeon, or a passenger the pilot of an aircraft. It means wholehearted commitment, with no reserve, no hesitation, no compromise and no small print. Do you believe with your will? The sixteenth-century Scottish preacher David Dickson described his own coming to repentance and faith in this way: 'I took my bad deeds, and I threw them on a heap; and I took my good deeds, *threw them on the same heap* and trusted wholly in Christ.' Notice the words I have emphasized! For many people, the major issue is not that of turning from obvious sin, but that of turning from the 'hidden' sin of trusting in what they claim to be their 'good deeds'. You dare not make the same mistake!

## Grace: found or forfeited?

The Old Testament statement we are examining records the tragedy of those who 'forfeit the grace that could be theirs', and I want to close by focusing on this phrase. 'Grace' means God's free, unmerited favour to sinners, something fine-tuned by the apostle Paul when he reminded early Christians: 'You know the grace of our Lord Jesus Christ, that though he was rich, yet for your sakes he became poor, so that you through his poverty might become rich' (2 Corinthians 8:9). Here is the very heart of the Christian gospel! Jesus left the glory of heaven, subjected himself to all the limitations of life on earth, allowed himself to be despised, abused and rejected, endured temptation of every kind and finally let himself be murdered by crucifixion, the cruellest method of execution then known to man—and he did it all so that undeserving sinners like you and me 'might become rich'! And how rich you could become...!

*Forgiveness of sins could be yours.* The Bible could not be clearer on this: 'Everyone who believes in him receives forgiveness of sins through his name' (Acts 10:43). You could be free from any fear of condemnation on the Day of Judgement, knowing that Jesus had paid in full the penalty you deserved.

*Peace with God could be yours.* Paul assured his fellow believers that, as Christians, 'We have peace with God through our Lord Jesus Christ' (Romans 5:1).

By nature you have a built-in hostility towards God and are exposed to his righteous anger, but if you put your trust in Christ the war will be over and you will have an inner peace that 'transcends all understanding' (Philippians 4:7) and that will remain even when faced with life's storms.

*Eternal life could be yours.* While sin brings physical and spiritual death, 'the gift of God is eternal life in Christ Jesus our Lord' (Romans 6:23). This means infinitely more than living for ever; it means doing so in a right relationship with God, enjoying his glorious presence, joyfully worshipping him face to face, rejoicing in his beauty and revelling in the spiritual blessings that he will shower upon you for ever.

*God's daily presence could be yours.* While eternal life is perfected in heaven, it begins for the Christian believer here on earth at the moment when he or she becomes a Christian. You would share the experience of millions of other believers who find that 'The LORD's unfailing love surrounds the man who trusts in him' (Psalm 32:10).

*Spiritual strength could be yours.* For all our self-confidence, there are times when we find ourselves unable to cope with sudden traumas or chronic pressure. As a Christian you will discover that you no longer have to face these things alone, that 'The LORD gives strength to his people' (Psalm 29:11) and that because you have a living relationship with Jesus Christ you will be able to draw upon his wisdom, grace and power day by day.

All of these blessings could be yours! Why forfeit them by trusting in 'worthless idols' that will shut you out for ever from the kingdom of God? Why settle for Polly Toynbee's bleak scenario in which 'no one is watching, no one is guiding, no one is judging and there is no other place yet to come … no one here but ourselves to suffer for our sins, no one to redeem us but ourselves…'?

I urge you to turn from this barren world view now, to fling all your 'worthless idols' away, to trust Jesus Christ as your Saviour and take him as your Lord while God in his patience and mercy is calling you to do so and it is still 'the day of salvation' (2 Corinthians 6:2).